MEGA-PREDATORS
OF THE PAST

Written by
MELISSA STEWART

Illustrated by
HOWARD GRAY

PEACHTREE
ATLANTA

Think you're looking at a dinosaur? Think again.

Sure, dinosaurs like *Tyrannosaurus rex* and *Giganotosaurus* were humongous hunters. And they did live a long, long time ago. But you know what? The last thing those supersized celebrities need is more attention.

That's why the stars of this book are prehistoric predators that had a whole lot in common with animals alive today—like this giant ripper lizard. Cool name, right?

We'll find out more about this tongue-flicking terror in a minute, but let's start with some mega-predators that look more familiar.

First up is a giant scorpion that lived more than 300 million years ago. Here it is, actual size. It was so huge it barely fits on this page.

The scorpion's strong, clawlike pincers were perfect for crushing insects and other small creatures. When a lizard scuttled by, the hungry hunter thrust its venom-filled stinger into the prey. *Zap!*

GIANT SCORPION

Mega Fact File

Pulmonoscorpius kirktonensis

Size: 28 inches (71 cm) long

Weight: 3 pounds (1.4 kg)

Discovery Announced: 1994

Discovery Site: Scotland

Lived: 345 to 330 million years ago

Wish you could see all the animals in this book at their actual size? Sorry, no can do. They're way too **BIG**!

But we've got something just as good—comparison figures. They'll show you exactly how huge the mega-predators were compared to humans and similar animals alive today.

Look at the size of that griffenfly!

1. Human | 2. Griffenfly | 3. Green darner dragonfly

GRIFFENFLIES

Mega Fact File

Meganeuropsis permiana

Size: 28-inch (71-cm) wingspan
Weight: Less than 1 ounce (20 g)
Discovery Announced: 1937
Discovery Site: United States
Lived: 290 to 248 million years ago

Griffenflies were closely related to modern dragonflies, but they were at least five times bigger. They had a long body and powerful wings. Their big eyes could see right and left, up and down—all at the same time.

When one of these hungry hunters spotted a *Paleodictyopterid*, it darted toward its target and caught the insect with its spiny legs. Then it popped the prey into its mouth and chewed the meal with its strong jaws.

What's next?

Terror birds! Their name says it all.

These terrifying titans hunted, well, pretty much anything they wanted to. Their closest living relative is the red-legged seriema, a more petite predator that lives in the forests and grasslands of South America.

1. Human | 2. Terror bird | 3. Ostrich | 4. Red-legged seriema

TERROR BIRDS

Mega Fact File

Kelenken guillermoi
Size: 10 feet (3 m) tall
Weight: 330 pounds (150 kg)
Discovery Announced: 2007
Discovery Site: Argentina
Lived: 15 million years ago

Terror birds were the biggest meat-eating birds of all time. They were too heavy to fly, but they had long, strong legs built to run. What was their top speed? Probably 30 miles per hour (48 km/h).

Nobody knows how terror birds killed their prey. They may have stabbed animals with their huge, hooked beaks. Or they could have picked up their prey and thrown it against the ground to break its bones. Either way, once the animal was dead, the mighty beasts enjoyed a feast.

Lucky for us, most of the gruesome giants in this book went extinct long before humans walked the earth. But not the short-faced bear. It lived right alongside our early ancestors. Just imagine what it would've been like to meet one of these burly bears in a dark cave.

1. Human | 2. Short-faced bear | 3. Grizzly bear

SHORT-FACED BEAR

Mega Fact File

Arctodus simus

Size: 11 feet (3.4 m) long
Weight: 2,000 pounds (900 kg)
Discovery Announced: 1854
Discovery Site: United States
Lived: 800,000 to 11,600 years ago

Was the short-faced bear really a predator? Good question.

Some scientists say, "Yes. Absolutely."

Others aren't so sure. They agree that the bear was a carnivore—an animal that eats meat. But a predator does more than eat meat. It also catches and kills its prey.

It's possible the short-faced bear stole prey from wolves, saber-toothed cats, and other smaller hunters. If that's true, it was a scavenger—not a predator.

It's also possible the bear was a predator *and* a scavenger. Sometimes it caught prey, and sometimes it stole food.

Here's another mega-mammal that scared the heck out of ancient humans. Look at the size of that carnivorous cat!

No doubt about it. American lions deserve some time in the spotlight. Why in the world do dinosaurs get all the hype?

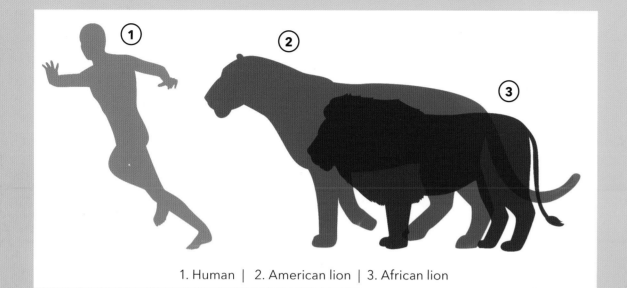

1. Human | 2. American lion | 3. African lion

AMERICAN LIONS

Mega Fact File

Panthera atrox

Size: 11 feet (3.4 m) long

Weight: 750 pounds (340 kg)

Discovery Announced: 1853

Discovery Site: United States

Lived: 340,000 to 11,000 years ago

Scientists know American lions were almost twice as big as the lions alive today, but they aren't sure how these prehistoric predators hunted. Did they ambush prey? Or did they chase it down? Did they hunt in groups, or did they hunt alone?

Researchers may not be able to answer these questions, but fossils do tell us what American lions ate—bison, horses, camels, deer, and even young mammoths.

Check out this giant turtle! *Archelon* was more than twice the size of leatherbacks—the largest sea turtles alive today.

You'll never guess where *Archelon* lived. Smack dab in the middle of North America. For 40 million years, a salty sea covered most of the land between the Rocky Mountains and the Appalachian Mountains. That's right! America's heartland was almost half a mile (0.8 km) underwater.

1. Human | 2. *Archelon* | 3. Leatherback sea turtle

ARCHELON

Mega Fact File

Archelon ischyros

Size: 13 feet (4 m) long

Weight: 4,800 pounds (2,200 kg)

Discovery Announced: 1896

Discovery Site: United States

Lived: 80 to 65 million years ago

Archelon had a wide, flat shell covered with leathery skin. It swam with paddle-like legs and caught prey with its powerful jaws. Like the sea turtles alive today, it probably dined on fish, sea jellies, and squid.

Even though *Archelon* was a mega-predator, it had enemies of its own. Because it couldn't pull its head or legs into its shell, it had to be on the lookout for supersized sharks.

Dive! Swish! Chomp! Gulp!

Meet the Sanders seabird—a prehistoric predator
guaranteed to make fish fret and squid squirm.
Besides being the biggest flying bird of all time,
it guzzled its prey with gusto.

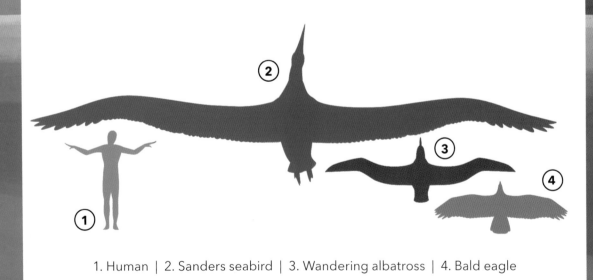

1. Human | 2. Sanders seabird | 3. Wandering albatross | 4. Bald eagle

SANDERS SEABIRD

Mega Fact File

Pelagornis sandersi

Size: 24-foot (7.3-m) wingspan

Weight: 90 pounds (41 kg)

Discovery Announced: 1983

Discovery Site: United States

Lived: 28 to 25 million years ago

The Sanders seabird had a wingspan longer than a pickup truck. To take off, it may have stood at the edge of a cliff and waited for a gust of wind to thrust it into the sky.

When the big bird spotted fish or squid, it swooped down and nabbed the prey with the bony, toothlike spikes lining its jaws.

Okay, we're back to the giant ripper lizard. This colossal killer makes Komodo dragons—the biggest lizards alive today—look like tiny tots.

Like most mega-predators, it had huge teeth and razor-sharp claws. But it also had a secret weapon—a powerful tail that could knock prey to the ground with a single blow. *Bam!*

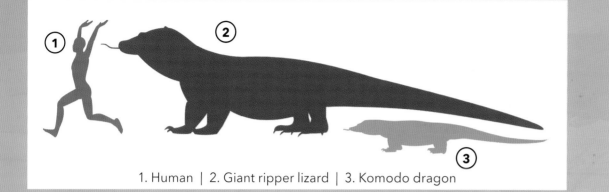

1. Human | 2. Giant ripper lizard | 3. Komodo dragon

GIANT RIPPER LIZARD

Mega Fact File

Varanus prisca

Size: 26 feet (8 m) long

Weight: 4,000 pounds (1,800 kg)

Discovery Announced: 1859

Discovery Site: Australia

Lived: 1.6 million to 40,000 years ago

The giant ripper lizard was twice as big as Komodo dragons, but it probably tracked prey in the same way—flicking its tongue in and out, in and out, to catch a scent.

Slowly, slowly, the hulking hunter snuck up on its target. And when the moment was right, it attacked.

As the lizard's teeth tore into wombat flesh, venomous saliva entered the bloody wounds. And when the prey stopped struggling, the mega-predator dug into its meal.

Hey, what's going on? That's *Albertosaurus*—a relative of *T. rex*. There aren't supposed to be any dinosaurs in this book.

Oh wait, it's the prey, not the predator. Ha!

Go, *Deinosuchus*! You've got this! That dinosaur doesn't stand a chance.

1. Human | 2. Deinosuchus | 3. American alligator

DEINOSUCHUS

Mega Fact File

Deinosuchus rugosus

Size: 36 feet (11 m) long
Weight: 7,600 pounds (3,450 kg)
Discovery Announced: 1909
Discovery Site: United States
Lived: 80 to 73 million years ago

This ancient alligator-like creature had huge teeth and a bone-crunching bite. It could have eaten just about anything that crossed its path.

Deinosuchus hunted underwater for fish and large turtles. And when a dinosaur came to the river for a drink, *Deinosuchus* launched a surprise attack. It sprang out of the water and grabbed the dinosaur with its teeth. Then it dragged the prey underwater and held on tight until the dinosaur drowned.

Think *Deinosuchus* was scary? Then you should probably shut this book right now. Seriously. Reading about a snake that's longer than a school bus might give you nightmares. *Titanoboa* was tough enough to catch and crunch crocodiles.

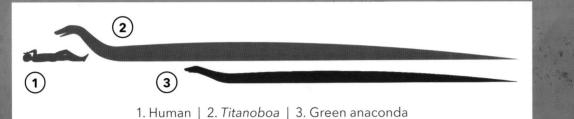

1. Human | 2. *Titanoboa* | 3. Green anaconda

TITANOBOA

Mega Fact File

Titanoboa cerrejonensis

Size: 43 feet (13 m) long

Weight: 2,500 pounds (1,100 kg)

Discovery Announced: 2009

Discovery Site: Colombia

Lived: 60 to 58 million years ago

Titanoboa was huge and heavy. It weighed four times more than the largest snake alive today.

What were the supersized snake's favorite foods? Large fish and small crocodiles. When the mega-beast spotted prey, it slipped silently through the water until it was close. Then it darted forward, grabbed the prey, and swallowed it whole. *Gulp!*

Still here? Then get ready for . . . *Megalodon*. This spine-chilling mega-predator makes the modern-day great white shark look like a guppy. The mighty meat eater was the size of a railroad car with teeth bigger than your hand.

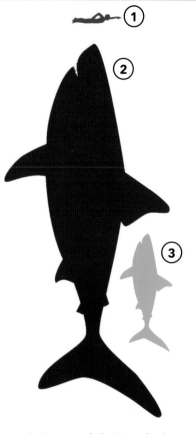

1. Human | 2. Megalodon
3. Great white shark

MEGALODON

Mega Fact File

Carcharodon megalodon

Size: 59 feet (18 m) long

Weight: 100,000 pounds (45,400 kg)

Discovery Announced: 1843

Discovery Site: Europe

Lived: 23 to 2.6 million years ago

What did *Megalodon* eat? Anything it wanted. Nothing stood a chance against the brutal beast.

When the hulking hunter spotted a whale or a dolphin or a giant turtle, it raced toward the prey at top speed. *Chomp!* The predator killed its target with one big bite. It could swallow chunks of meat as big as a horse.

But *Megalodon* wasn't the biggest predator of all time. Not by a long shot.

And believe it or not, the world's most massive meat eater is still with us today. The blue whale is twice the size of *Megalodon*, and it makes *T. rex* look like a puny pipsqueak.

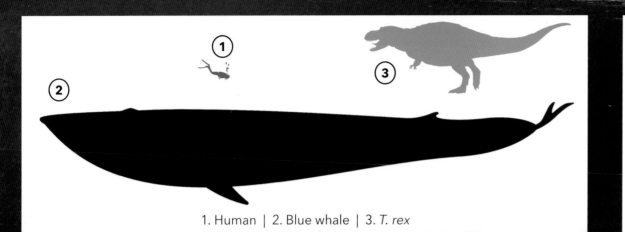

1. Human | 2. Blue whale | 3. *T. rex*

BLUE WHALE

Mega Fact File

Balaenoptera musculus

Size: Up to 110 feet (33.5 m)

Weight: Up to 330,000 pounds (150,000 kg)

Discovery Announced: 1694

Discovery Site: Scotland

Lived: 3 million years ago to today

A blue whale may be huge, but it eats tiny shrimplike creatures called krill.

How does the mega-predator catch its prey? First, it opens its mouth wide and gulps in gallons of water full of krill. Then it shuts its mouth and uses its huge tongue to push the water out. Thousands of krill get caught in comblike plates called baleen, and the whale swallows them. It can eat as many as forty million krill in a day.

Face the facts, friends. Snarling, stalking, scene-stealing dinosaurs are overexposed and overrated. It's time to let other prizeworthy predators of the past share the stage.

COMPARING MEGA-PREDATORS BY SIZE

Sanders seabird

Megalodon

Giant ripper lizard

American lion

Deinosuchus

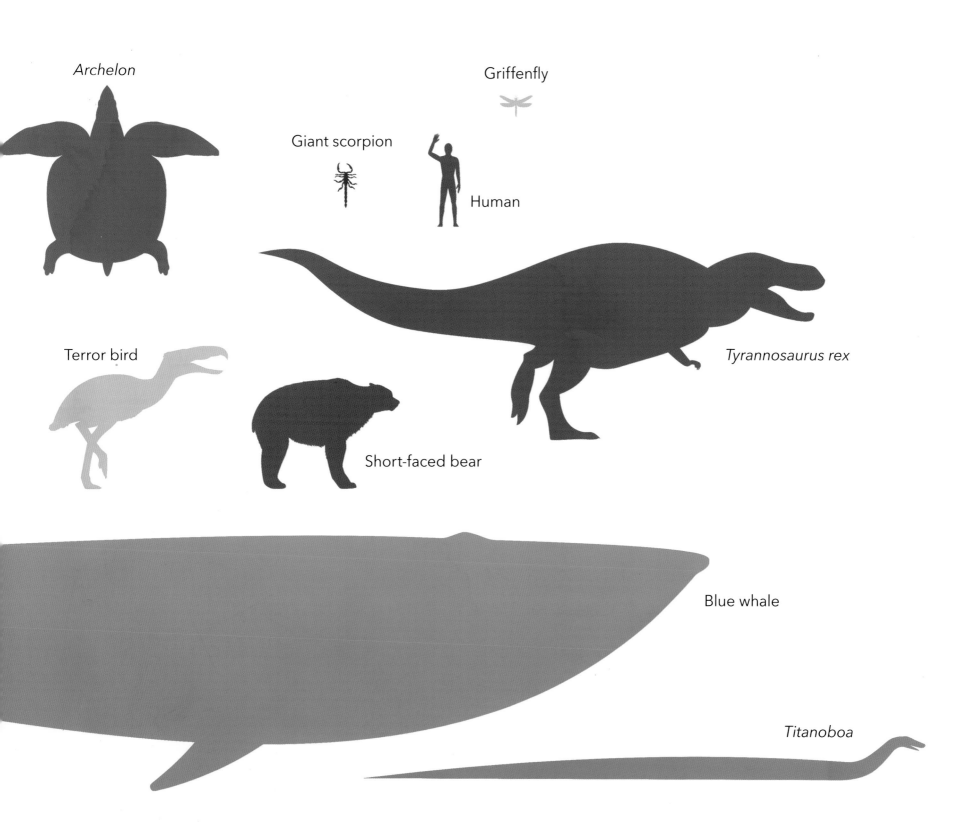

Archelon

Griffenfly

Giant scorpion

Human

Terror bird

Short-faced bear

Tyrannosaurus rex

Blue whale

Titanoboa

Author's Note

As I dug into the research for this book, I found a lot of contradictory facts and figures. How was I supposed to decide which sources were the most reliable?

First, I looked at where and when the information was published. Scientific articles are often more accurate than books, and recent sources usually have the most up-to-date information. I also considered the author. How knowledgeable were they? What kind of sources had they cited in their bibliography?

In some cases, I had to learn more about the specimens scientists were studying. Were researchers working with full skeletons or making estimates based on just a few bones? Were they using living animals to predict how ancient ones looked and acted? If so, did that approach make sense?

I also had to find out whether there were competing ideas about a particular mega-predator. Did most scientists agree about the size of an animal and how it hunted and what it ate? Or were there two or more different theories?

What did I learn during this research process? Figuring out what ancient creatures looked like, how they behaved, and when they lived can be tricky. And sometimes scientists just don't have the answers—at least not yet.

In many cases, I was able to wade through the research and feel confident that I'd found the most accurate and up-to-date information. But sometimes I wasn't sure. That's when I tracked down experts and asked for their help. I'm grateful to the scientists who patiently listened to my questions and helped me find answers. The information in this book is based on the best research available at the time it was written. But who knows what we'll discover in the future. That's what makes science so exciting.

—Melissa Stewart

Illustrator's Note

Did American lions have manes? What kind of environment did griffenflies live in? These are some of the many questions I set out to answer when illustrating this book. It was not always easy to find the answers.

My focus was on how the animals (and their prey!) looked and, to an extent, how they behaved (e.g., did individuals hunt in groups?). Various artists have portrayed these creatures, but when possible, I consulted the continuously growing body of scientific articles and books that investigates them. I searched for information about the kinds of environments these animals occupied, including the plant species that were around at the time. Virtually everything we know about these animals comes from fossils and specimens, so I also made sure to study photos, drawings, and descriptions of the species described in the book. One interesting resource was cave paintings. How incredible that our ancestors were around to document some of these amazing creatures! Occasionally, I picked the brains of fellow scientists who happened to know a bit about a particular predator, or the geological time period associated with it.

Where I couldn't find the answers I needed, I took a really good look at an animal's closest living relative. This was often a great way of filling in any gaps, such as the color of an animal's fur. Only occasionally did I need to make an educated guess, and when I did, I wanted it to look believable (yet visually interesting)—which was fun to do, of course!

—Howard Gray

Selected Sources

Bertelli, Sara, Luis M. Chiappe, and Claudia Tambussi. "A New Phorusrhacid (Aves: Cariamae) from the Middle Miocene of Patagonia, Argentina." *Journal of Vertebrate Paleontology* (August 2010): 404–19.

"Extinct Short-Faced Bear (*Arctodus* spp.) Fact Sheet." San Diego, CA: San Diego Zoo Wildlife Alliance Library. 2021. https://ielc.libguides.com/sdzg/factsheets/extinctshort-facedbear.

Goforth, Chris. "A Long, Long Time Ago, in a Galaxy…Well, Right Here." *The Dragonfly Woman*, August 22, 2011. https://thedragonflywoman.com/2011/08/22/giant-insects.

Gugliotta, Guy. "How *Titanoboa*, the 40-Foot-Long Snake, Was Found." *Smithsonian Magazine*, April 2012. http://www.smithsonianmag.com/science-nature/how-titanoboa-the-40-foot-long-snake-was-found-115791429.

Hamers, Laurel. "Fossil Whale Hints at Baleen Makeover." *Science News* (June 2017): 12–13.

Head, Jason, Jonathan Bloch, Jorge Moreno-Bernal, Aldo Fernando Rincon Burbano, and Jason Bourque. "Cranial Osteology, Body Size, Systematics, and Ecology of the Giant Paleocene Snake *Titanoboa cerrejonensis*." *Society of Vertebrate Paleontology* (October 2013): 140–41.

Hu, Jane C. "The World's Largest Flying Bird." *Slate*, July 7, 2014. https://slate.com/technology/2014/07/worlds-largest-flying-bird-pelagornis-sandersi-had-a-24-foot-wingspan-lived-in-south-carolina.html.

Jeram, Andrew J. "Scorpions from the Viséan of East Kirkton, West Lothian, Scotland, with a Revision of the Infraorder Mesoscorpionina." *Transactions of the Royal Society of Edinburgh: Earth Sciences* (1994): 283–99.

Neuhauser, Alan. "Largest Ever Flying Bird—a Prehistoric 'Dragon'—Discovered." *U.S. News & World Report*, July 7, 2014. www.usnews.com/news/articles/2014/07/07/largest-ever-flying-bird-a-prehistoric-dragon-found-in-south-carolina.

Prehistoric Life: The Definitive Visual History of Life on Earth. New York: Dorling Kindersley, 2012.

Richardson, Hazel. *Dinosaurs and Prehistoric Life*. New York: Dorling Kindersley, 2003.

Wheeler, H. Todd, and G.T. Jefferson. "*Panthera atrox*: Body Proportions, Size, Sexual Dimorphism, and Behavior of the Cursorial Lion of the North American Plains." *Museum of Northern Arizona Bulletin* (January 2009): 423–44.

For Further Reading

Arnold, Caroline. *Giant Shark: Megalodon, Prehistoric Super Predator*. New York: Clarion, 2000.

Jenkins, Steve. *Apex Predators: The World's Deadliest Hunters, Past and Present*. Boston: Houghton Mifflin, 2017.

Jenkins, Steve. *Prehistoric Actual Size*. Boston: Houghton Mifflin, 2005.

Woodward, John. *Dinosaur! Dinosaurs and Other Amazing Prehistoric Creatures as You've Never Seen Them Before*. New York: Dorling Kindersley, 2014.

To Vicky, for her endless patience and unwavering
dedication as we created this book.

—M. S.

For my dad

—H. G.

Acknowledgments

We are grateful to the following scientists for sharing their time, expertise, and passion for prehistoric life with us.

- Brusatte, Steve, Chancellor's Fellow in Vertebrate Paleontology, School of GeoSciences, University of Edinburgh, Edinburgh, Scotland
- Dunlop, Jason, Curator of Arachnids and Myriapods, Museum für Naturkunde, Leibniz Institute for Evolution and Biodiversity Science, Berlin, Germany
- Erickson, Gregory M., Professor of Anatomy and Vertebrate Paleobiology, Florida State University, Tallahassee, Florida
- May, Mike, Professor Emeritus, Department of Entomology, School of Environmental and Biological Sciences, Rutgers University, New Brunswick, New Jersey